SPEAKING IN CODE
PHODISO MODIRWA

Published by Akashic Books
©2023 Phodiso Modirwa
ISBN: 978-1-63614-132-9

Akashic Books
Brooklyn, New York
Instagram, Twitter, Facebook:
@AkashicBooks
E-mail: info@akashicbooks.com
Website: www.akashicbooks.com

African Poetry Book Fund
Prairie Schooner
University of Nebraska
110 Andrews Hall
Lincoln, Nebraska 68588

TABLE OF CONTENTS

PREFACE
by Tsitsi Jaji

Speaking in Code introduces an arresting new voice in African poetry from Botswana. While anchored in the specific ground of her own location, it is precisely Modirwa's poetic voice that shows us how an individual's being in the world exceeds the limits of language. The images and word choices are lucid, and metaphors are wonderfully sustained throughout entire poems. We are never in doubt of the poet's control of craft; a strong current pulls us through harrowing experiences of harm, survival, and the ambivalent zones in-between, but the collection also fulfills its title's promise, speaking in poetic code.

Without a doubt, Modirwa's code will challenge readers. Occasional Setswana is sewn into the English, sometimes in passing, elsewhere as the driving force of the poem. But more importantly, the messages in these poems are deftly rendered opaque, sheltering the healing underway through a multiplicity of meanings that only metaphor and the play of space on the page can achieve. In a poem early in the collection, she turns the expectation for simple answers ("filling an application form for my national id") into a series of questions, miniature self-portraits, and testament to her relationship with her mother. Rather than the state's privileging of a father's name, Modirwa roots her identity in a legacy of women's struggle: "i came tumbling down between her relief and joy. i was born in her survival."

The collection is propelled by what the poet tells us is "a war inside myself," angered by the depths of suffering she wishes "not / to remember." And yet her carefully crafted verse does something far more powerful than forget, it transforms pain into a fierce testimony to the imagination's generative capacities. The layers of loss Modirwa exposes and undoes are perpetrated by patriarchy, domestic violence, and corrupted church institutions that invent "a cowardly god," alternately blind and hostile to what exceeds reductive oppositions. Modirwa's faith in the word is shattering, and she asks us to rise to its occasion. Her language is in touch with a written legacy in search of burning bushes that can't be found, and in her hands its poetics refuses resolution but speaks life into the perpetual challenge of ciphering. This poetry shows us the intricate topologies of thought emerging from elegantly spare word choices that churn familiar images into unsettled possibility:

> in this one line   lives
>   the inside out of this poem
>   my blood—a red sea that won't part
>   for my crossing.

("red sea")

This is a poet who knows Biblical language from the inside out and lives in the wildly human dimension of shifting perspectives, certainty in revolt. Imagine with Modirwa, for instance, the version of Lot's story where a husband confesses to his wife: "I am a coward of a man /returning only now to the ruins of your heart's chambers" and recognizes that her glance back home was an act of bravery, facing "the thing that would unmake us." ("lot's account")

Like her fellow Botswanan, the great Bessie Head, Modirwa captures the psyche in distress with startling empathy. Throughout the collection these poems play with voice and standpoint, and in several of the final poems we find the intimate attention of one reflecting on a sister's sojourn through a psychiatric hospitalization. What does it mean to stay close to the anguish of an involuntarily committed sister, aware of the deep sorrows that have driven her out of her right mind, noticing the gaps between her perceptions and what we think we know as reality, to hear her longing for home as well as the fear of what that homecoming will feel like? As the collection draws close to kin, it allow us to hear a drifting between first and third persons. We listen in on the sister's monologue and then glide back into the concerns with motherhood that opened the collection. The vulnerability of pregnancy finds its obverse in "mis /carriage," a loss so often written off, or rather, too rarely memorialized. Time and space drift into each other, and a walk through villages translates the nine months not reached.

Modirwa's meticulous language strikes a ceremonial tone throughout, and shows us that the true power of poetry is the elemental transformations rendered by each act of imagination. Closing with the most fundamental questions – *"who are you?"* and *"where are you going?"*—*Speaking in Code*'s answer is these very pages. How fortunate we are to dwell on these words.

MY FATHER IS NOT

i want a world in which my father is not
a vengeful god who might give food
but then kick the plate for grace not said

a world in which i don't have to beg
my sanity at the altar of a father's love
in the name of prayer or sacrifice

i couldn't feign piety that way
or worship at the temple of a god fallen
all tantrums and anger for blessings

a world in which papa is not
a flickering flame and i
some moth desperate for the light

FILLING AN APPLICATION FORM FOR MY NATIONAL ID

i) *name*: mother, is this the part where i tell our story packed tight into one word?

ii) *surname*: this is the space my father could have sat in but he was away when they named me. so mother gave me her grandfather's, said it will do between now and the time a man tethers me to himself like a branch. till i want kids with him to add to this shrub of a family tree.

iii) *gender*: this one time a family member said i should have been a boy because, *what's with the hairstyles and legs as far apart from each other as men's ways from god's?* i didn't think it made any difference when all i ever saw was women asked to sit down while men did with their legs as they pleased: stood, ran, danced. if i sit down, will that tell you?

iv) *nationality*: i don't know. you mean within which borders i belong? as in where i will always be from even if i leave for years and years? i belong to a country whose descendants came here running from battles, *mfe-cane* is the first i learned of. sometimes, where i come from, something might blast loud and bright and even in the face of that danger, we wear our curiosity like running shoes to go see what would be so brave to try to end us. i belong within these fearless borders.

v) *date of birth*: there are twenty reasons inside the five that made nineteen ninety-two a song. the five, poetry, solitude, questions, questions, questions. it was in the dusk of autumn.

vi) *place of birth*: the story goes my mother was so deep into the desert when her water broke it was the only thing that saved her—her water. i came tumbling down between her relief and joy. i was born in her survival.

i swear that the information i have provided is true to the best of my knowledge.

please sign on the dotted line

……………………………………..

this space is small and the questions dug too shallow. so let me say, i was born running away from a war inside myself to my mother's side of the family. sometimes when i'm sleeping, i can feel the violent gallop of a small animal running fast and past me. i would have become a man but i'm still a girl.

RED SEA

my father angers   me.
        in this line   lives   the rest of the poem,
in my blood   what i wish not
             to remember.

        i was born—   a violent   awakening,
    then took a nap   through the pocket   of childhood.
awakened again
           by my mother's   silence,
    held tight   by the grip of her lover's
                violence.
we left that egypt
        by way of emang basadi.

    o what a longing   we had
           for a moses whose sandals
                we'd not seen
at our door post,   who'd not found us—dried up
           branches in a burning bush
but returned   to watch *muvhango*   with his family
    because   he heard
      a cowardly god say
           nothing to see here.
    my father loves   me,
in this one line   lives
        the inside out of this poem
my blood—a red sea that won't part
        for my crossing.

WASTING AWAY

on the day of our mock exam,
       everything is a mockery.
after sliding between my teeth the fat 50t coin
       with the fish eagle holding a fish,
i mean, holding me, where its feet end your hands begin.
       my whole being, prey to a father who will take what he can from
the water without letting it touch him.
       i wait with bated breaths to touch your voice from gaborone,
so heavy and safe if the call lasts.
       my classmates speak of your old age, say–
rraago ke monnamogolo akere?
       a forced glance at the hourglass needing a turn.

       through the years i try to love a man my mother couldn't reach.
            i'm holding an eagle rapturously escaping my embrace
                in the end,

a couple of feathers in my hands and enough
       cuts to warrant a kind of leaving,
i pack my love back into heart.
       i let myself quiver between strangers in the back of a taxi
on my way home telling a sister it hurts, my god, it hurts
       so bad, to love a man who won't love you back—
who will wipe the kiss of you off his mouth
like a vice he isn't too proud of.

       it is a decade and more years later,
            we don't have any more time than we did back then
                and the man still won't let me in.

though he loves to see me wait outside his barricaded heart,
loves to see me pine and ache,
    loves to see this love waste away like our days.

TRAVELERS

    to return to him   is to return to an egypt
without the garlic   or the onions—
       without flavor or sustenance   so what for?
she is her own
       kind of moses
         traveling
           down
              the desert of her depression.
   holding her two daughters,   a staff on each side—
     she says   keamogetse   and hasn't she accepted her plight?
she says phodiso and   it is a flickering prayer
               blazing through the night.

    two decades ago
         they left her husband's house,
two decades   later   they are still travelling
       away.

SPEAKING IN CODE

of sweet culprits offering pleasantries
in houses their wives make home—
their bloodied wives
with amputated courage so they cannot fight back

    my mouth is a locked door
    the keys? swallowed, like a pill—
    a thing to numb the pain
    my body placeboed into oblivion
    sometimes silence looks like healing
    look the part; fake it till you make it

        i don't talk about the thing that marred
        my body reckless
        made an apparition of me in the air
        i cannot call it love though it was a thing
        like it at first
        not the kind to maroon even a small animal

            but i am speaking aren't i
            which means the door is open; you can come in
            if you find blood spluttered on the fridge
            assume someone was slaughtering an unwilling chicken
            no animal with blood pulsing warm in its veins goes
            down without a fight
            but i swear, the blood is not mine

                if you find a limb atop the tv
                it is an ornament; assume it was severed

from a really tired tree—it said thanks
but i swear, the arm is not mine

you are the visitors
and i am not pleading with you not to leave
i am not begging you to lower me through
the window of your compassion out of this house

see? i am not bloodied
my body misses no limb
you're having a nice conversation
with my sweet-sweet husband
and i am not saying
you're looking my killer in the eyes

EXORCIST

the man with the black suit is coming to my house today   mama told
him i act like a boy   she says she will not mother abomination
not while her spirit commands her body the man says this can be fixed
the man plays exorcist and pours oil over my head   the man
                                         touches the oil
flowing down my neck   the man does not stop

inside my too small bedroom it is just i and him his hands do not stop
he speaks in a language no one uses at home   after this mama tells
me i'm free   i want to tell   someone   what the man did
how his hands made my body   something to be explored   a map
in braille   but my heart beats   the courage out of my mouth
my tongue unfurls and i stutter   mama tells me to stop playing
with words   and all the language in my mouth finds a place to hide

the man with the black suit is coming for dinner tonight   the
                                      man with the
black book is saying grace in my house   my eyes are wide open
he sees me   through the deception he has cast like a web over
my parents   sees me   through the eye he has for little girls
like me   this eye is a wandering thing hungry and ugly

i lose my voice   to gain it back seven years after the man's *amen*
the man says *amen* and all the glasses in the house shatter   all the
bibles swallow their god and i have nothing   to pray to

CALL IT WHAT IT IS

pelonomi's curtains   are drawn   all day,
every passing eye   makes spectacle   of her.
the mundane   duty   of making   the bed,
the private-now not-task   of standing   in the shower
then reading   a book over cold tea,   undressed.
the neighbors   are   complaining,
our children's   *innocence is being*   *defiled.*   at church
they say   the body is   a temple   yet some men
fear no god.   at evening time   when
the drapes of darkness   fall,
let them see   what has been taken,   she says.
surely there is nothing   sacred   here,
yes   the men   came,   took
what they   wanted.
on the heels   of their leaving i ripped   curtain   off rail,
here,   i said to the world,
take   whatever   remains.
they   think they have   a name   for it now,
for us   the plundered.   will see it   as anything but
a desperate attempt   at agency,
call it   sexual liberation,   hyper   sexuality
or call it what it is—

trauma

INFERENCE—AFTER SAFIA ELHILLO'S VOCABULARY

the setswana word *tlala* means hunger
the setswana word *tlala* means full

> the little girl said   *ours is a house of deprivation*   or
> the little girl said   *ours is a house full*   *of absence*

> the girl knows hunger   and
> the girl knows pretense

the setswana word *tatolo* means denial
the setswana word *tatolo* means obituary

> mmapula says   *here lies the man's denial*
> mmapula says   *here lies the man's obituary*

> mmapula speaks of gaslighting   and
> mmapula never gets justice

you could say *bua* to mean speak or
you could say *bua* to mean slaughter

> mojadi says *nnaka, speak for me*   or
> mojadi says *nnaka, slaughter for me*

> mojadi is asking for advocacy   or
> mojadi is asking for retribution

SHAPE SHIFTING

it is an obsession i know / this turning of my words into grackles
against the night sky of imagination / like an eagle i attempt flight
focused in the eye of the storm and unafraid / but i am afraid i can-
not fly / i am a disappointment to my mother in that i am still afraid
of the dark / but in my dreams i visit graveyards of trauma / scatter
the church of tombstones standing like pious guardians over memory
/ a cross here for the crossroads of twenty-three / when i relive my
grandmother's falling into the mouth of a dead animal and so be-
came it / a brick for my father here as duplicitous priest shepherding
memory into forgetfulness so that i forget what came first—me or my
doubt / a rising up into a time when the last page of revelations turned
and there was still no canaan for our sojourning / just open desert /
my mother's water breaking / my sister and i paddling silly like swans
in the wrong direction / her hard labor at stuffing that curious gut of
childhood with more promises / sister, i try to keep up but with every
blink our mother shifts into a palpable metaphor / flash! the woman
is a veil before our eyes / attempting though failing to eat the light
of our sight / flash! the woman is a church and we are new converts
singing negro spirituals like love songs / flash! the woman is a god and
aren't we devout / the woman is prayer and us, her resounding amen /
the woman is an altar and every day we come to say the sinner's prayer
/ we are sinners here / the woman is the only prayer bead left after the
cathedral caught fire / the woman is a garden and us, blooming chry-
santhemums of christ without the doctrine / without the command-
ments / without the anointing oil and fasting / without doubt her own
/ full and missing nothing

LOT'S ACCOUNT

i know
i am a coward of a man
returning only now to the ruins of your heart's chambers
my eyes are a gaping mouth taking everything in
but you are not here my love
save for your defiance monumented into a pillar of salt
i want to say i forgive you to mean i understand
for what mother doesn't look back at a home she built
while penance eats at her heels saying *leave*
leave your house
leave your children
i watched the holy halo of birds circling your head while you turned
i am sorry i was not that brave
not enough to face the thing that would unmake us
please borrow me your god
i promise to tend to him like a lamb
his bleat my command
maybe then he will let me in on where your soul rests
maybe then i too will know rest from ruin
in another bible story there is no god
hurling plagues for blessings
there is only the pheromone of another wafting richest farther away
      from home
or maybe there is a god and i am not his chosen one
if you know not what whittles a man to bone though he keeps return-
      ing to the line
you know not the beguiling ways of that other woman
she licks her lips
the animals are whipped to quick feet and i fall beside her

lightning strike!

MY SISTER ASKS ME TO KEEP THE LIGHTS ON

when i call her the next week she does not recognize my voice / she is
an old moth outliving its ambition for the fire / but she is not out of the
woods ablaze and thirsty for the whiff of something in her breath / she
says she is sorry-not-sorry but it is not my fault / like that will lift like
morning the weight of loss over me / she says she does not get the point
of her room in which she stands holding the bars like a caged animal /
i don't tell her it is for her own good / last week she emptied the petrol
bottle into her mouth and spent the day slipping off the oily hands of
consciousness / when she called me, she was a smoldering wick afraid of
the darkness eating its last flicker / her will to live—smoke wafting into
the unknown night / my words—charred out matchsticks of short-lived
hope/ the call for the emergency services—a savior who still couldn't
bear her cross / she writes

> you are your own until you try to not be / then you're the state's
> / the neighbor's / your mother's / guilt howls like a wolf from
> inside the darkness you tried to vacate / calls you back into it /
> like it will keep the lights on inside of you / can you keep the
> lights on for me?

MY SISTER WRITES FROM THE HOSPITAL SHE CALLS PRISON

sister did you know? prison is a locked door / it thinks the only way to save you is to shut you in / it is a hand reaching out to pull you out only / you don't want to be saved / not like that / not inside steel walls cold with reasoning

in prison, the other inmates tunnel their way like worms into your mind / ask you why / tell you you're so pretty which sounds like, *you have imaginary problems* / in prison, the guards who should be nurses hover like birds around you / with droppings of opinions you didn't ask for

prison is a daylong rhythmless song / is the sanitized voice of a distant woman telling you *it is okay* / she is so kind but the walls aren't / she is so kind but the walls aren't

sometimes prison is a house on fire / they say the fire will burn out the thing that tried to make you leave but i am the one burning / to talk to anyone outside is to cup my body like a tongue and receive whatever bead of water their care is / do you see me panting?

MONOLOGUE IN WHICH MY SISTER IS AFRAID TO COME HOME

i'm just afraid i will come out
and will belong to a time so forgotten

i will have to forgive
anyone who thinks me a myth

i am afraid i will rattle my loved one's peace
with my creaky joints rusty from neglect

when i followed the melody of the black raven
i couldn't leave anything so much as a note

i do not find fault with their setting sail without me
i was a weight too heavy even for my carrying

i have been kneading myself into a lump
of something salvageable but i am just afraid

i will come home when everyone's favorite tv
program is on— during the last episode of *prison*

break or *how to get away with murder*
and will make everyone miss the end

AFTER THE PSYCHIATRIC WARD; *BOTSETSI*

sabrana
that sterile dish with sides so slippery i couldn't climb
up the walls to see outside
i learned to hold my breath under water unlike fish
bridled—more like a brute beast perhaps
for a month i lay on my back and felt the cold wet
and desperate discomfort of a strangeness coming
like a new baby falling out slowly from her first home

and when i heard a cry rising up in my throat
i leaped the leap of a mother's instinct seconds before
her little one turns in sleep to be startled
by the floor's urgent violence
but the shackles around my limbs rattled to remind me
trust was a long way from there

*

i am back home now and crying most days
afraid for this new fragile thing i have brought
back home
a kind of apparition i need to feed on patience to keep
alive
to one day have it walk back into me—sanity

i want myself back but the doctors said to slow down
said this is just like *botsetsi*
a kind of maternity aftercare

MIS / CARRIAGE

my life is a walk all day through pouring rain

i think i missed it—the party carriage
going farther down by the ninth village
where all the women arrive belly in front of them
and return arms full with fruition
i have known this third village as both delay and loss

i am a tree with branches for hands but i cannot hold
one single fruit till it ripens

i carried it wrong
maybe i came inside from the torrential rain
wrung myself so tight i lost my grip on everything
even on the last hope of motherhood
i always return by the third village
all empty hands and tired body
with nothing to show for my journey

INHERITED PURSUITS

you did not come to die here did you?
saddled to a horse that knows no halt
to your mother's back in her pursuit
of something far away from here
even seed knows it is both demand
and promise trudging the vast fields
of reason like from here could also
come a treasure

you have inherited your mother's quick
legs   her flight-for-fight make of a heart
at the end of this journey the horse is a
unicorn   you knew this was a dream
how else would you have gotten here without
the labor?   you're looking for home
have only your name as a compass

north nothing here is yours, not even your
name
south something is calling you into a search
you have not packed up for
east   everyone believes you when you say
you have arrived
you say it because you're tired and did not
carry enough water for the journey
west   where have you chosen to lie and call that
place home?

have you too accepted this lonely sojourn

as yours?　　the way your mother accepted
the long travel of servitude for the quench
of your father's affection?　　are you a pilgrim
in your own body?　　hoping for a mecca of
answered prayers

inside your borrowed campus of a name
you cannot sit still enough for any precise reading
the cardinals are arranging themselves to ask
who are you?
where are you going?

ACKNOWLEDGMENTS

"filling an application form for my national id"—*Ghost City Review*

"exorcist"—*Jalada 08: Bodies*

"wasting away"—*20.35 Africa: An Anthology of Contemporary Poetry*